The Coral Reef
A Giant City Under the Sea

by Stephen Person

Consultant: Rod Salm
Coral Reef Ecologist and Director of
The Nature Conservancy's Marine Conservation Program
in the Asia-Pacific Region

BEARPORT
PUBLISHING

New York, New York

Credits

Cover and Title Page, © Bruce Coleman/Photoshot; 4-5, © Morozova Tatyana/Shutterstock; 6TL, © Maximilian Weinzierl/Alamy; 6TR, © Reinhard Dirscherl/Mauritius/Photolibrary; 6B, © Prisma/SuperStock; 7, © Mark Evans/iStockphoto; 8, Courtesy of Rod Salm; 9T, © Jurgen Freund/Nature Picture Library; 9B, © World Travel Collection/Alamy; 10, © Chris Newbert/Minden Pictures; 11L, © Bruce Coleman/Photoshot; 11R, © Pacific Stock/SuperStock 12T, © Adam Butler/Alamy; 12B, © David Fleetham/Nature Picture Library; 13T, © Andre Seale/age fotostock/SuperStock; 13B, © Masa Ushioda/Alamy; 14, © Jodi Jacobson/iStockphoto; 15T, © Fred Bavendam/Minden Pictures; 15B, © Fabio Liverani/npl/Minden Picures; 16-17, © Zeynep Mufti/iStockphoto; 17, © Courtesy of Scott Santos/NOAA; 18, © Burnett & Palmer/age fotostock/SuperStock; 19, © SeaWiFS Project/NASA Goddard Space Flight Center/Orbimage; 20, © Jeff Rotman/Nature Picture Library; 21T, © Jurgen Freund/Nature Picture Library; 21B, © Pacific Stock/SuperStock; 22, © frantisekhojdysz/Shutterstock; 23, © Michael Patrick O'Neill/Alamy; 24, © Paul Palau/Courtesy of Rod Salm; 25, © Australian Institute of Marine Science/Reuters/Landov; 26T, © Roland Seitre/SeaPics.com; 26B, © Flip Nicklin/Minden Pictures; 27, © James D. Watt/SeaPics.com; 28T, © cbpix/iStockphoto; 28M, © Adrian Baddeley/iStockphoto; 28B, © RHePhoto/Shutterstock; 29T, © Tim Laman/National Geographic Stock; 29B, © Willem Kolvoort/Nature Picture Library; 31, © Morozova Tatyana/Shutterstock.

Publisher: Kenn Goin
Editorial Director: Adam Siegel
Creative Director: Spencer Brinker
Design: Dawn Beard Creative
Photo Researcher: James O'Connor

Library of Congress Cataloging-in-Publication Data

Person, Stephen.
  The coral reef : a giant city under the sea / by Stephen Person ; consultant, Rod Salm.
    p. cm. — (Spectacular animal towns)
  Includes bibliographical references and index.
  ISBN-13: 978-1-59716-869-4 (library binding)
  ISBN-10: 1-59716-869-6 (library binding)
  1. Coral reef animals—Habitations—Juvenile literature. I. Salm, Rodney V. II. Title.

  QL125.P45 2010
  578.77'89—dc22

                        2009012952

For more information, write to Bearport Publishing Company, Inc., 101 Fifth Avenue, Suite 6R, New York, New York 10003. Printed in the United States of America.

10 9 8 7 6 5 4 3 2 1

Contents

Color and Action

As a young boy, Rod Salm first saw a **coral reef** while swimming in the ocean near his home in Mozambique (*moh*-zuhm-BEEK), Africa. "It was confusing," he remembers. "There was so much color and so much movement and so many different creatures doing different things. It was hard for me to take it all in."

Today, Rod is a coral reef scientist. He studies reefs all over the world, from Hawaii to the huge Great Barrier Reef of Australia. He is still amazed by the color and action he sees. "Schools of jewel-colored fish dart quickly in and out of cracks in the reef," he says. "It's like nothing at all found on land."

Coral reefs are found in the **coastal** waters of more than 100 countries.

Cities Under the Sea

Rod Salm says that exploring a coral reef is like visiting a magical city under the sea. Just like most human cities, coral reefs are **diverse** places. In fact, coral reefs are the most diverse **habitats** in the ocean. They are home to more than one million **species** of fish, plants, and other sea life.

Picasso triggerfish

Trumpetfish

More than 4,000 different kinds of fish, including the triggerfish, trumpetfish, and coral grouper, live in and around coral reefs. New species of reef fish are discovered each year.

Coral grouper

The Great Barrier Reef is the biggest reef in the world. It stretches for more than 1,400 miles (2,253 km) along the coast of Australia. This reef is home to 1,500 species of fish. It also has more than 5,000 kinds of **mollusks**, such as clams and oysters. When scientists studied one basketball-size chunk of coral there, they found 103 different species of sea worms!

The Great Barrier Reef (shown below) is not a single reef. It is made up of about 3,000 reefs. Parts of the reef extend 100 miles (161 km) from the shore.

Reefs cover less than 1 percent of the ocean floor. Yet they are home to almost a quarter of all the plant and animal species in the entire ocean.

The Buildings Are Alive!

Coral reefs look like groups of colorful buildings rising up from the ocean floor. However, reefs are unlike human cities in one important way. The buildings are alive! Reefs may look like rocks, but they are actually made up of the skeletons of small animals called coral **polyps**.

Coral reefs, such as this one, are often made up of many different species of coral. There are more than 750 different types of reef-building corals in the ocean.

Coral polyps look like tiny **sea anemones**. They have tube-shaped bodies with a mouth at the top. Around the mouth is a ring of stinging **tentacles**. Polyps use these tentacles to catch food and chase off other animals, such as sponges, that try to grow on top of them. Polyps also protect themselves by building cup-shaped stony skeletons around their bodies and living inside them.

Most coral polyps are very small—less than one inch (2.5 cm) tall. They usually live for two to three years.

a coral polyp's tentacles

cup-shaped skeleton

Sea anemone

Coral polyps are related to jellyfish and sea anemones. All animals in this group have tentacles that can sting, so divers need to be careful when they swim near these sea creatures.

Slow-Growing Cities

How can tiny coral polyps build huge underwater cities? The answer is: very slowly. When adult polyps **reproduce**, they release **larvae**—the young form of coral polyps. The larvae drift until they find a hard surface to settle on, such as a rock or the skeleton of a dead coral. The larvae then grow into polyps, staying in the places they have settled until they die.

These polyps have settled on the skeletons of dead corals.

a coral polyp

skeletons of dead coral

As they grow, young polyps form stony skeletons around their bodies. The polyps divide and build new skeletons around themselves, leaving the old ones behind. In this way, a **coral colony** is formed. Each colony can have thousands of polyps. When many coral colonies grow close together, a coral reef is formed.

Elkhorn coral

As coral colonies grow, they take on many different shapes. Some species look like antlers, others look like mushrooms or brains.

Brain coral

Because each coral polyp is so small, corals usually grow less than one inch (2.5 cm) per year. Most coral reefs today are between 5,000 and 10,000 years old.

Busy Days, Busy Nights

Just like big human cities, coral reefs are very busy places. During the day, fish circle the reef in search of food. The parrotfish uses its beak-like mouth to eat polyps and coral skeletons. When it releases waste, the fish deposits the ground-up skeletons as sand. Much of the white sand on **Caribbean** beaches is formed in this way.

A parrotfish eating coral

A single parrotfish can produce one to five tons (.9 to 4.5 metric tons) of sand each year.

A parrotfish releasing a cloud of sand made up of coral skeletons it has eaten

There's even action around the reef at night. While the daytime animals tuck themselves into the reef's cracks to sleep, the nighttime ones come out to feed. Coral polyps reach their stinging tentacles out of their skeletons to catch tiny floating animals called **plankton**. Night is also when **predators**, such as octopuses, lobsters, and big fish, come to the reef to hunt for **prey**. To escape, small fish dart into the reef's cracks.

The coral polyps' tentacles sway in the water as the polyps feed during the night.

Large predators, like this reef shark, come to the reef at night to hunt for fish.

Depending on Each Other

Thousands of animals and plants live in and around the coral reef's underwater city. Yet they don't just live with each other. They depend on one another to survive. Together, they make up the coral reef's **ecosystem**, which includes water, sunlight, and coral polyps, as well as all the animals and plants living in and near the reef.

Clownfish stay safe in coral reefs by swimming close to sea anemones—which can sting the clownfish's enemies.

A clownfish can swim among a sea anemone's tentacles without getting stung due to mucus that covers the fish's body. In return for a safe place to live, clownfish drive off animals that want to harm anemones.

"The creatures of the reef all contribute to the growth and health of the coral reef community," explains Rod Salm. For example, some fish help the reef by eating seaweed that grows on corals. This gives new corals a clean place to settle and grow. In turn, the nooks and crannies in a coral reef provide a safe place for fish to hide when they see predators coming.

Moray eels hide in cracks in the reef. They stick their heads out to catch fish as they swim past.

Turtles come to the reef to tuck themselves under a ledge and sleep.

The Smallest City Residents

Algae are also part of the coral reef ecosystem. Some of these plant-like **organisms** reach up to two feet (.6 m) tall. Others are so tiny that thousands of them can live in just one polyp. Don't be fooled by their size, though. Without algae, coral reefs could not survive. Why?

Algae make their own food. They use the sun's energy to turn water and chemicals in the water into things like sugar. Coral polyps also need to eat this food—or they will die. The plankton they catch are not enough to keep them alive. Coral polyps give algae a safe and sunny place to live in return for providing food.

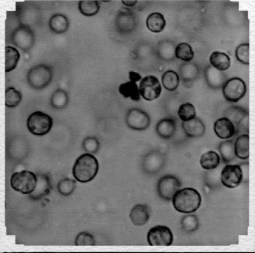

This is a close-up image of algae in a coral polyp. These algae are so small that people can see them only with the help of microscopes.

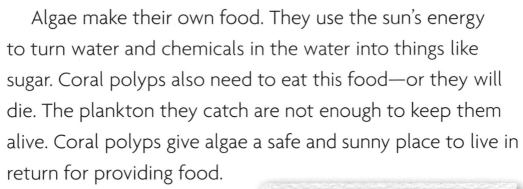

Algae come in many colors, such as green, red, yellow, and pink. The color of the algae is what gives corals their bright colors. Coral by itself is white, similar in color to human bones.

Warm Water and Sunlight

Coral polyps need the tiny algae inside them to survive, and algae need strong sunlight to make their food. For this reason, coral reefs cannot grow everywhere. Deep or cloudy water does not allow enough sunlight to reach the coral polyps and algae. As a result, coral reefs grow best in areas with clear water that is less than 150 feet (46 m) deep.

These corals in the Great Barrier Reef grow in clear, shallow water.

Coral reefs also need warm water, with temperatures between 70°F and 85°F (21°C and 29°C). This is why reefs are found in **tropical** waters. The Great Barrier Reef grows in the warm waters along Australia's eastern coast. Coral reefs are also found along Central America, East Africa, many Pacific islands, and other tropical areas.

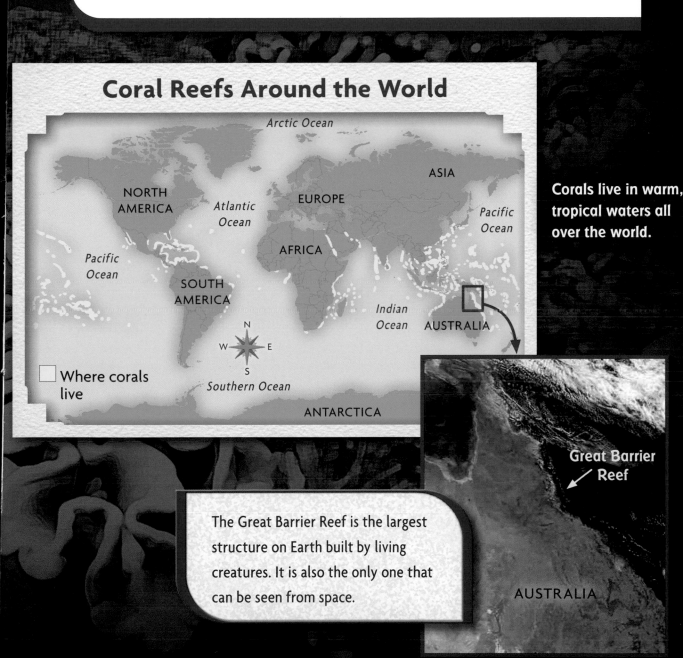

Coral Reefs Around the World

Arctic Ocean

ASIA

NORTH AMERICA

Atlantic Ocean

EUROPE

Pacific Ocean

AFRICA

Pacific Ocean

SOUTH AMERICA

Indian Ocean

AUSTRALIA

N
W   E
S

Southern Ocean

ANTARCTICA

☐ Where corals live

Corals live in warm, tropical waters all over the world.

Great Barrier Reef

AUSTRALIA

The Great Barrier Reef is the largest structure on Earth built by living creatures. It is also the only one that can be seen from space.

Why We Need Reefs

Coral reefs aren't just beautiful to look at. They are also helpful to people. Some of the plants and animals in reefs are used to make medicines that fight diseases like cancer and heart disease. In addition, millions of people rely on the fish that live in coral reefs for food.

These fish were caught in a coral reef.

Coral reefs also help create jobs for many people. For example, more than one million tourists visit Australia each year to explore the Great Barrier Reef. Australian workers serve as tour guides for these visitors, rent and sell them diving equipment, and work in the hotels that visitors stay in. This tourism has created more than 60,000 jobs in Australia.

People come from all over the world to scuba dive and snorkel at the Great Barrier Reef.

About 500 million people around the world rely on coral reefs for food and jobs.

Fragile Ecosystems

While people rely on coral reefs in many ways, they are also often a danger to them. For example, people sometimes create water pollution that can harm the reefs. How? If trash is not thrown away properly it can be swept by storms into rivers. The rivers then carry the trash to the sea. When garbage floats in the ocean it can block sunlight that algae need to make food for themselves—and for coral polyps.

Coral reefs are very fragile. Swimmers and divers can damage them just by stepping on or touching them.

Another threat comes from people who use **explosives** to catch fish. When fishers throw an explosive onto a reef, it **stuns** nearby fish. This makes them easy to catch. However, it also destroys large areas of a coral reef.

Scientists are working to convince people not to use explosives to catch fish at coral reefs. This reef in Indonesia was destroyed by explosives.

Danger: Warming Waters

The greatest threat to coral reefs is the changing **climate**. Human activities that involve the burning of oil, coal, and gasoline release gases that trap heat in Earth's **atmosphere**. This can cause Earth's air and ocean water temperatures to rise.

Scientist Rod Salm studying the health of a coral reef

Warmer water is not good news for coral polyps. They are sensitive to even small temperature changes. When temperatures rise, coral polyps often release the algae that live inside them. Without algae to make food for the polyps, corals can starve to death.

"We could lose many coral reefs by the end of the century," warns Rod Salm. However, "there is hope for corals if we act now to protect them."

Without colorful algae, coral becomes white. This change is known as "coral bleaching." Bleached coral can recover if water temperatures return to normal.

Scientists believe that about 30 percent of the world's coral reefs have been destroyed in the past 30 years. They warn that another 30 percent of reefs may be lost in the next 20 years.

Protecting Coral Reefs

To protect coral reefs, many countries are turning the areas where corals live into **marine** parks. Oil drilling and damaging fishing practices are not allowed in these places. Australia's Great Barrier Reef Marine Park covers an area larger than Great Britain. In 2006, the United States set up a huge marine park to protect the coral reefs of Hawaii.

Bottlenose dolphins are one of many species that live in the Great Barrier Reef Marine Park.

The Hawaiian monk seal is one of the species that is protected in Hawaii's coral reefs.

Rod Salm believes that we can all do our part to protect reefs. When swimming near them, it is important not to "bump, break, or stand on corals," he says. Instead, "slowly float over them." By protecting reefs in this and many other ways, people can make sure that these magical cities beneath the sea continue to thrive.

A bluefin trevally swims in a coral reef at Papahānaumokuākea (*pa*-pa-hah-now-moh-*koo*-ah-KEH-ah) Marine National Monument in Hawaii.

The Papahānaumokuākea Marine National Monument covers nearly 140,000 square miles (362,598 sq km) in Hawaii. That's larger than all the U.S. national parks on land put together!

Coral Reef Facts

Coral reefs are built by tiny animals called coral polyps. Coral polyps are closely related to jellyfish and sea anemones. Here are some more facts about these tiny builders.

Size	Most polyps are from .25 to 1 inch (.63 to 2.5 cm) wide. Some grow as wide as 12 inches (30.5 cm).
Colors	red, pink, yellow, brown, blue, orange, purple, or green
Food	plankton and sugar made by algae
Predators	parrotfish, crown-of-thorns starfish, worms, snails
Reef Growth Rate	usually about 0.2 to 8 inches (0.5 to 20.3 cm) per year
Habitat	warm, shallow, clean ocean water along the coasts of Australia, southern North America, South America, Africa, Southeast Asia, and tropical islands
Life Span	Polyps usually live about 2 to 3 years, though some species can live much longer.

More Animal Towns

Coral is not the only animal that builds underwater colonies. Here are two others.

Sea Squirts

- Sea squirts are tunicates (TOO-ni-kits), a type of sea animal with a firm, flexible covering called a "tunic."
- Most sea squirts measure from .04 to 2.4 inches (0.1 to 6 cm) in length. They feed by filtering bacteria and plankton out of the seawater that they "squirt" through their bodies.
- Young sea squirts resemble tadpoles. They swim through the ocean and eventually attach themselves to hard surfaces, such as rocks or ship bottoms.
- Sea squirts form colonies by attaching themselves to a hard surface very close to one another.

Bryozoans

A bryozoan colony

- Bryozoans (brye-uh-ZOH-uhnz) are tiny animals that can be seen only with a microscope. They live in both freshwater and seawater.
- Bryozoans live in colonies of up to millions of individuals, each of which forms a protective skeleton.
- Colonies settle on hard surfaces such as rocks, pipes, and wooden docks.
- After forming a colony, bryozoans do not move. Members of a colony perform different tasks, such as collecting food or defending the colony.

Glossary

algae (AL-jee) plant-like organisms that grow in water or on damp surfaces and make food using energy from the sun

atmosphere (AT-muhss-fihr) the mixture of gases that surround Earth

Caribbean (kuh-RIB-ee-uhn) having to do with the Caribbean Sea, located between North and South America

climate (KLYE-mit) the typical weather in a place

coastal (KOHST-uhl) having to do with the land that runs along an ocean

coral colony (KOR-uhl KOL-uh-nee) a large group of coral polyps

coral reef (KOR-uhl REEF) a group of rock-like structures formed from the skeletons of sea animals called coral polyps; usually found in shallow tropical waters

diverse (dih-VURSS) varied

ecosystem (EE-koh-*siss*-tuhm) a community of plants and animals that depend on one another to live

explosives (ek-SPLOH-sivz) devices that blow up

habitats (HAB-uh-*tats*) places in nature where plants or animals normally live

larvae (LAR-vee) the young form of some animals, such as coral polyps

marine (muh-REEN) having to do with the sea

mollusks (MOL-uhsks) animals with no spine and a soft body, usually protected by a hard shell

organisms (OR-guh-*niz*-uhmz) living things

plankton (PLANGK-tuhn) tiny animals and plants that float in oceans or lakes

polyps (POL-ips) small sea animals, such as coral, that have tentacles and a round mouth

predators (PRED-uh-turz) animals that hunt other animals for food

prey (PRAY) animals that are hunted or caught for food

reproduce (*ree*-pruh-DOOS) to have offspring

sea anemones (SEE uh-NEM-uh-neez) brightly colored sea animals with tube-shaped bodies and tentacles

species (SPEE-sheez) groups that animals are divided into according to similar characteristics; members of the same species can have offspring together

stuns (STUNZ) shocks something so much that it is unable to move

tentacles (TEN-tuh-kuhlz) long, arm-like body parts used by some animals for moving, feeling, or grasping

tropical (TROP-i-kuhl) having to do with the warm areas of Earth near the equator

Bibliography

Chadwick, Douglas, H. "Kingdom of Coral: Australia's Great Barrier Reef." *National Geographic* (January 2001).

Coral Reef Alliance. "About Coral Reefs." www.coral.org/~coralorg/resources/about_coral_reefs

National Oceanic and Atmospheric Administration. "What Are Corals and Coral Reefs?" www.coris.noaa.gov/about/what_are/

United States Environmental Protection Agency. "Coral Reef Protection." www.epa.gov/OWOW/oceans/coral/

Read More

Bingham, Caroline. *Coral Reef.* New York: DK Publishing (2005).

Galko, Francine. *Coral Reef Animals.* Chicago: Heinemann (2003).

Gibbons, Gail. *Coral Reefs.* New York: Holiday House (2007).

Learn More Online

To learn more about coral reefs, visit
www.bearportpublishing.com/SpectacularAnimalTowns

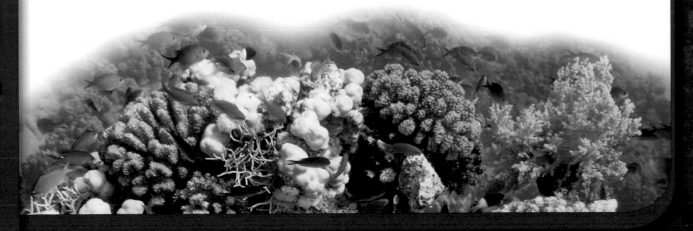

Index

About the Author

Stephen Person has written many textbooks, as well as children's books about the environment, nature, and history. He lives in Brooklyn with his wife and daughter.